A TREE BECOMES A ROOM

A TREE BECOMES A ROOM

J.P. White

WHITE PINE PRESS / BUFFALO, NEW YORK

White Pine Press
P.O. Box 236
Buffalo, NY 14201
www.whitepine.org

Publication of this book was supported by public funds from the
New York State Council on the Arts, with the support of Governor
Kathy Hochul and the New York State Legislature, a State Agency.

Acknowledgements: Many of these poems have appeared in:
*Bodega, Leaping Clear, Woven Tale Press, Heartland Review, Willow Springs,
American Journal of Poetry, The Georgia Review, The Great River Review,
Miramar, Mudlark, Salamander, Catamaran, Poet Lore, Gris-Gris, Cloudbank,
The Briar Cliff Review, Plant-Human Quarterly, Salt, Humana Obscura,
Pensive, Talking River Review, Tusculum Review, Flint Hills Review, Peripheries*
and *Sequestrum.*

I'd like to thank my dedicated readers including Neil Shephard, who
has seen everything I've written for forty plus years, as well as Jay
Hornbacher, Lynn Armstrong, Sally White King, Willow King, and
Kat White, who has made all the difference in my life and work.

Book Design: Elaine LaMattina

Printed and bound in the United States of America.

ISBN 978-1-945680-65-6

Library of Congress Control Number: 2022950766

CONTENTS

For Jim Moore
& for Kat

DREAM OF A LOQUAT

Somewhere in the upper curl of the Italian coast,
I am leaning over a rampart
to pick a darker shade of orange gold loquat.
It's a long way down to the sea.
I reach for a simple truth:
Some fruit is worth a fall.
This one, sweet and tart at the same time.
This one, out on a high branch with a view of the harbor
and the anchovy boats that have just returned.
I tell myself I am so close,
it should be mine to pick.
I am old by now with my arms outstretched
and my fingers grasping.
It seems all I can do is hold this moment forever.

FOUR SILVER CRANES

Not everything was better in the past.
Not the truncheon, the knife, the rope.
Not the seas torched with oil and blood.
Not the ones who dealt in slaves, broke treaties,
and laughed at the ones down on their knees.
That list is long enough so we can stop now
and remember instead the trout streams
snaking between Wyoming and Montana,
the blues bars in Cleveland with gin and eggs
served after the last set, summer nights in Sonoma
tasting the ocean mist free of smoke,
the fat jade crickets singing after midnight
without knowledge they will be devoured at dawn
by the meadowlarks once so thick
you could stroke their feathers.
I would like to go back
to the tortoise-shell butterfly meadow of an earlier year,
and I would like to stay here inside this ruin,
where we lay down on the earth, thanking her
for making room for us, who met late in years,
and now here we are looking up
at four silver cranes on a figure eight,
their set and glide a gateway into the upper room of this once only.

THE SOUND OF ONE RUSSIAN NAME
IN MY EAR

I

When I told our host Luba I had pus and blood draining from
    my ear,
and I couldn't board a plane in such a condition and return
    to Minneapolis
with our daughter, all that way, how many time zones,
holding my head in a handkerchief, she said,
In Russia, we don't go to doctor even if we are dying. You are pathetic.

You would have been hard pressed to find anyone
who knew less about an infant. Nothing about
feeding and changing. Nothing about how to soothe her.
Though I had no skill, I wanted to be able to hear her,
so I told Luba I was pathetic
and I needed her help to find a doctor.
She shook her head and we went off in a cab
and I found a doctor from the West
who claimed to have escaped from America
after a malpractice suit blew up. To get there,
he flew his own plane under radar and landed
outside Moscow, then stole a bicycle.
He loved the raw wild of the place.
Loved how all you had to do was keep the Mafia happy.
I'm not sure he ever looked at my ear.

II

The mad cab ride all turned out according to humble plan:
I got drugs that day. Luba and I shook hands.
My then wife and I adopted a daughter
from an orphanage In Nizhny-Novgorod and we got a plane.

III

She almost never calls me now, but she does text often.

My ear has never been the same. It can't be fixed.

Vera means faith in Russian. Truth, in Latin.

Vera, one of three martyred saints, whose portrait
is found on key chains, on books,
above light switches, in churches and cemeteries
everywhere in Russia, this girl, this name, abiding.

Vera means I can drive all over Moscow
with a Russian woman who thinks I am pathetic.

Vera means I can still hear a daughter crying
in a train station where dirt-covered mushrooms
and tiny red apples are spread out on a tunnel sidewalk.

Vera, the story of all my listening. Long ago and now.

Most days I will say her name to myself just to hear the sound of it.

The Taming Power of the Small

What does Heaven have to say? Help everything.
Help the ant and beetle navigate the kitchen.
Help the bearded iris seek the fat loam.
Help the lovers pause at the lighthouse.
Help the general gain a view from the coffin.
Help the child retrieve the goat from the monkeypod.
If you have any question about how to spend your day,
it's of some comfort to know, isn't it,
that everything needs help to cross a bridge,
put down a sword, walk away from a sadness.
You never have to look far for something
that needs a way out or a way in.
When my hands reach for you in the night,
I think you will come to me willingly,
but what do I know of your location?
Which is when I tell you about this
lime-colored moth I caught and escorted
to the door. What a battle it was.

SMOKE

After the tumor had been cut from his throat
and the radiation had started to cheat his swallow,
he told me how in the long middle of a winter night
in Ward C, he got up craving a smoke,
even though he no longer smoked
and he walked down a hall with his IV pole
to a fire escape so he could stand outside
and pretend he had gone there to draw on a cigarette,
and once there it started to snow,
and at first he didn't see the other man
who had come there for the same reason with his IV pole,
but then through the expanding steam of breath,
it became clear my friend was not alone.
He was not startled but instead started talking
with the other would-be smoker
as if this sudden gathering was a normal outing for both of them.
The other man said he was dying of lung cancer
and my friend said he'd had his last rites
read three times and maybe he was already dead
but the fact had not yet sunk in.
The two men stood on a fire escape in St. Paul, Minnesota
and shared something in that unlit place
and I picture them now, wondering
if they met again after they were gone
for by the end of their winter talk during a snow fall,
they swore they would talk soon and often.

THE WORLD AS IT IS

So many worlds to take seriously.
The world of baby steps.
The sudden late fall off a curb.
The world of the spear, the shield,
and that one pink grandiflora rose
that throws down the hint of a siren perfume.
The world where, on her birthday,
our 36-year old daughter
steps into Crosstown Gas & Convenience
on the 5700 block of 34th Avenue in Minneapolis
to grab a pack of cigarettes
just a minute after a shooter opened fire.
The world where it's unclear
whether the shooter knew who he wanted to kill
or whether he only took out a bystander.
The world where the manhunt has now begun in earnest,
where mortgage rates are too damn high,
jets roar over rooftops night and day,
and where Kelsey, with her wife at the stove,
is now making a ginger stir-fry with veggies from a raised bed.

THAT'S HOW THE DAY BEGAN

The older I get, the less sleep I need.
At this rate, I will soon start my days like I did
when I was a baker in the first reach of the flour bin.
Always unsettling to drive down the canyon
in the pitch, praying a deer would not collide
with my wheels. That's how the day began.
Thinking about death and derailment beside the road.
Then, inside my hands, the brightening
of another world in the shape of donuts, Danish,
French braided loaves, rye and wheat.
Some long-chained molecule of me is still there
with the dark of the grocery store
all around me like a moat, putting my palms to work
in the gold shade of brushed egg and the ovens
just beginning to throw off a warmth.
Still wanting to feed myself, to feed others.
To feast on some secret of the universe
that begins in the switchback
of a dangerous road, solitude, bread in my hands.

VERONICA, OFFSEASON

We had been staying in a lemon grove above the sea.
In a guesthouse with a deck.
Impossible, the beauty and the quiet.
Over wine, we launched clever schemes for how to stay there.
We had come long before the flood of tourists
would arrive by train from Milan.
Before the heat would make hiking
a hard ladder in the lungs.

Many nights, we danced naked outside, laughing.
Like that, children again.

Below us, the village of anchovies and mimosa.
Above, an abandoned monastery
and the stations of the cross on the climb up,
each a diorama set back in rock.

I remember your saying,
Everything belongs in the window.

And Veronica with her handkerchief,
she was there at the sixth station wiping his face.

Once we were alone with the lemons, grapes and Veronica.

Outside of love, we die even faster than we already do.

Splash

I will spend part of this day thinking of the companion animals
who have found me
on some mountain or out in the ocean
or just down the street near the sprawl of purple lilacs.
Part of this day in the shade of their welcoming,
when I could not welcome myself.
Part of this day thanking them
for showing up when I needed them most,
even the ones who hissed, snarled or stole my food.
All of my riddles will remain unfinished
or unsolved, but not theirs.
The fox will sliver a fire beyond the last fence.
The nightingale will summon the lovers back to bed.
The wasp will live again on the point of a dagger.
The turtle will sip the champagne air.

I will spend part of this day thinking of the dogs, geese, dolphins,
donkeys, pigs, cats, goats, horses, whales and sheep
that have befriended me
and then vanished before we could finish our conversation.
Like that mother bear who slipped across the St. Vrain River
        at dusk
with an apple in her mouth,
but who waited to swallow till her three cubs had made the splash.

When We Sit Down to Eat,
We Sit Down with the World

What things offer good news to the world?
Trees and dogs. Stars over the desert.
The fox emerging out of her winter hollow.
The iron skillet hanging above the stove.
Cilantro, sage, parsley and rosemary
are hard to fault. The lovers are divided.
Half are enthralled. The other half require
vigil and reassurance. War, a given:
the revolt of the rich against the poor
has not changed in two thousand years.
You can still hear crickets setting up camp
at the far edge of the over-lit city
and my spoon scraping the bottom
of a pot I've used since I was twenty.
When you tell me to add extra garlic
and basil to the soup, I know I can manage
the knife of your wish. When we sit down
to eat, we bless our food, the day we met,
this life together. When you open
your eyes to look at me, I will open mine.

In My Old Address Book,

You will find lawyers who will be chained to a bed of nails in
        the afterlife,
my first minister who heard ee cummings at Harvard
read from his *six nonlectures*, my sailing crews,
my neighbors who befriended or failed me,
musicians, florists, real estate agents who I torched
looking for a cottage on a dead-end street,
former wives, rectal specialists, harbor masters,
mechanics who never quit on a knock and a rattle,
a psychic who invited me to Kenya to listen to lions mating,
little hotels on the Île Saint-Louis, directions
to a box canyon in Sedona where petroglyphs
have not yet been tattooed by witless hikers.

Near the back yellowing pages,
where the spine shows a tearing away,
there you will find the many apartments of my sister Anne White,
who never laid claim to more than a nickel,
and who looked like a top-knot Chinese scholar
before she died with a smile that swept over great distances
with a lightness that made her famous
among the bird call residents at her last stop nursing home,
a picture I drew of her face in the marginalia,
her smile still true at the end as if she knew
that most of what we do here is move around,
plead our case, make mistakes, get sick, ask for help.

Finding a Child's Swing Hanging from a Jacaranda in a Cove Below a Lava Field During the Time of Sickness

It's like this everywhere.
It takes time to see something.
Time to worm beneath the shard of a small agony,
sit there all day and eat of it.
Time to get lost in the remote corner of a monologue
you started with yourself in a previous century,
then zigzag home.
Almost everything gets more interesting
when you leave the trail
and never open the map.
Like when we followed that thread of beach
and found a child's swing in a cove
strung from a jacaranda.
Everything about this place was familiar
and nothing felt safe
near the upwelling of ocean in the lava.
We took off our clothes, played near the water.
Slept between each other's legs.

I forgot that time is always the tiger shark in the aquarium.
That a cloud is a reef of a thousand fish.
Whether it was afternoon or evening when we left.
How many strings of purple flowers fell on our heads.

Can We Please Keep the World Out of Our Bed?

I will leave this life without understanding
the unobstructed reach of the army
or the king's command to kill the Holy Innocents
or why I gave decades to the captains of industry
in return for my little stack of chips.
I will barely get anything right about the serpent or the dove
or how we got this far with greed as our guide.
If I have any honesty left, I will confess
to my contributions to the landfill
and how I could I have done more or a great deal less.

Until then, I have one request:
that we make of our bed a wilderness to keep the world out.
No pings. No TV. No podcasts.
No more dissections about our imminent collapse.
Just us doing all we can not to be reached,
and you without your blue dress on,
the two of us navigating by ridge and valley and there, a river
            to cross.

Paper Box Kite Launched from Captiva

That night, with the wind ragged enough to lean against,
Vera and I watched revelers coaxing
a paper box kite to climb,
their song to it buffeted by the slap of waves.
Such a difficult birth
for this stringless kite crabbing over sand,
the candles rocking, a burst and a guttering
as if already heavy with the worries of the flesh
and the threat of decomposition.

Then the slow lifting
and the light of it a quickening,
then gone over the rough blue face of salt.
How could I tell her, at sixteen, this was enough,
more than enough,
this lick of flame, this flicker, with a second storm coming on?

Two Sisters at Crist Mortuary

She kisses the fallen sister where she lay in a cardboard box.

She places photographs, flower petals and letters
on her body, kisses her again.

A shine on the skin where the lips touch.

Not a hair of your head will perish, says Luke.

I can see them there in that antechamber,
in the garden incorruptible,
waiting for whatever comes next.

Two sisters in a moment of devotion.
Then, the door opens.
One sister releases the other into flames.

Dread and glory. Her hand lifting for a wave.

Just a Little Bit of Rain

That's all it takes for the wilted purple milkweed to return
    from the dead.

For the stubborn leaves in a besieged heart to rattle a high thin
    branch.

All it takes for the oldest basement rock called Vishnu schist
    to touch

a cloud, for the dry river bed born a thousand years ago to feed

a tooth of corn, just a little bit of rain is all it takes for the umbrella
    man

to appear again and tell that joke about the chicken at the gym
    looking

to beef its neck. I could join the others and say everything has gone
    too far

and there is no coming back from this game called, *Waiting for the End,*

but here's what I've seen from my decades in the dirt and
    on the water,

all it takes is a little bit of rain for the scorpion to climb out
    of the boot

and for the fixed idea to put down its sword. Water flicking a face,
    the tears

that click the tongue, and the land will drink all night from just a
    little bit of rain.

DRIFT

Nothing is going to get better and everything today is perfect.

First, walk to the fruit seller, the one with a necklace

of garlic on his cart and let him hand you a bag of loquats.

Second, find again the elderly sisters swimming way out

beyond the cove and try to calculate again the geometry

of their ridiculous, long-distance, dog-paddle breaststroke.

Call this a luxury, this morning drift with a string bag

of stone fruit or call it something else, a zigzag skip,

a riddle, a pledge to the cosmos. Third, I will look around,

grateful for everyone in the play, the ones who steal,

cheat, lie, gulp expresso, make love, get old, suffer, gasp,

laugh, and light a candle for everything they can't hold.

OLIVE TREE ON ITHACA

What else craves the stint of slowness?
The bumblebee ass up in the bucket of a rose.
The infant stalled at the door of the womb.
The dying can sometimes take longer
to round the track
than it took for Odysseus to reach Ithaca.
Which brings me to the olive tree on that island
believed to be the oldest of the old.
Here when Constantine saw in Christ
the last chance to unite the scattered empire.
Here for the guillotine and for Mozart.
Here with me now.

Hard to trust the slow work of mercy
when we can't agree on the terms of our pathology.
Harder yet to trust a god
ruled by lust or the need to punish,
but easy to sit with this ancient one
fat as the bow of a warship.

Nothing really happened in our time together.
Another blistering day
during the last inconclusive days of quarantine,
a sail in the distance, no more than the nick of a triangle.

BEAUTY AT THE TABLE

It's easy to imagine how everyone who has ever been born
has failed the earth
just by turning away from some ancient crime,
and now we know the cost even if we can't speak of it,
but this other matter of beauty,
the thrill and pleasure inseparable from the brevity,
who doesn't need something or someone to help them build
a bridge to carry them to the other side
of some lostness or isolating hunger
and find it one more time?

Said another way:
the table is set down at the river's edge.

The arrangement of apricot lemonade cosmos,
scabiosa and chocolate lace flower are brought out
and you can hear what happens next
with some voices too soft, others a little too loud,
then a sigh, an exclamation,
and a sense that the long-awaited summer dinner can now begin.

Vultures Over the Immigrant

As much as I complain about vultures circling the immigrant
and the pecan trees failing on the hill,
I don't ever want our time to end.
I can't imagine entering the vast warehouse of the dirt
and the thought of flame makes me dizzy.
Even on summer days, I'm not especially keen
on saying goodbye to anyone.
I will never make a good Buddhist at my winter dojo
traveling the long dark with that question,
What is my death asking of me?
When I'm asked to be a eulogist,
I say I'm honored, then I hide in the basement.
I have never once embraced the notion
that death must sit down for dinner
in order to make breakfast possible.
Most days, my love, it's hard for me to remember
that everything bears fruit,
everything I have loved and fought for, everything
I have rejected, despised, turned away from,
everything here sings for a time
from the little shining of its birth no one saw coming.

WHAT WE SAID WE DIDN'T NEED,
WE FOUND MORE OF

The gypsy moth, the cane toad and bark beetle
do not require apology or condolence.
The tiger shark, not on the verge of vanishing.
The centipede will make out like a bandit.
They will probably all bear the trials
by fire and flood and find a room at the inn.
On the other hand, we can expect more stones
from the sky, smashed mirrors, expulsions,
scribbled signage, the flash of knives.
And what else awaits us here?
I remember driving in Provence, thinking
it was so hot, nothing could breathe,
nothing could live here, nothing
until I found the heaven of stone fruit
set out in baskets in the shade of umbrella pines.
Cherries, plums, peaches, nectarines, apricots.
I swerved often, my mouth
spilling over with fleshy sweetness.
One farmer after another looked worried
by the spatter-glow of teeth,
my chin dripping with juices.
I was now that blinding riddle caught by the sun.
A reptile parked at the side of the road.
A prince of the grateful, expectant heart.

The Clouds Will Be Living Longer

Almost everything we are now told is on the edge of the last edge.
The bluebird, the red oak, the crocodile holding
a single egg in her jagged teeth.
But here's something else you can bake into summer:

The big, fat, wandering clouds that forever follow
the lust of youth and the complaints of age
and all the trials of the earth that never end,
the clouds that provided
your first glimpse of the zoo animals,
and that regard every seed in the ground as companion,
those same clouds that have been traveling the earth
since before you were born
and will be wantonly lazing on the day of your death,
those clouds will be gathering more rain, more power, more wind.

When almost everything else is failing or fallen
and even the stones in the road are threatened,
the clouds you have always regarded as your animal friends
will know what to do and how to get there.

The Elephant in the Kitchen
as the Future Buddha

While breaking open two cubes of yeast for dinner loaves,
I had it explained to me by a child
that long before he sat under the bodhi tree and said
any one of us is only one blink away
from seeing everything,
he too struggled here for a time.
A hundred thousand eons, more or less.

In one of his early incarnations,
He was an elephant.
What kind? I ask her.

Before I brush the braided loaves with butter
and slip them into the oven
so the entire house will gather in the balm
of yeast, flour and flame,
she asks me to picture this gray cloud of hunger,
rummaging a midnight kitchen,
tearing through walls with its tusks,
bowls and plates shattering in the mill of voracity,
the gristle pad of each heel smacking the floor,
the eyelashes of the elephant flicking away the dust,
an entire house shaking
with a terrible need for the lift of sugar, the thrill of salt.

THE BUTTERNUT TREE

On and on, the tongue keeps a lookout for the jagged tooth,
and the bright axe of the world speeds
through the yellow light thinking this time it won't be late
and now little is heard from the crested honeykeeper.
But what if the broken wing of some old story
had no authority to carry me back,
what if the river was the only voice in the kingdom?
My questions went on and on like that
until I entered the old curl of sleep (if you can call it that)
and I woke again in a spill of light
that had made out of our bed a softness,
an invitation, a boat facing a new day
and you said, the butternut tree has never looked better.

LITTLE PIG CROSSING

road sign in Hana

After the evening closing of the Da Fish taco truck,
four piebald pigs who live in the orchid roots
scuttle the one road keen on scraps.
The darkness gathers a stronger weave
without the reach of streetlights
and the night is what it has always been,
an empty sleeve for starlight.
Avocados, bananas, coconuts, guava
and papaya are all roadside free.
A machete left on the stump.
A wooden bowl for donations.
The pigs go there for dessert.
Even though this scene could be gold leaf
on an onyx jar,
the earth would be better off without us.

Lapin

This business with a knife and fork is bound to get more
      complicated.
Who knows what will be on the menu next?

As the world enters more fire swaths
and the fox and coyote fall to the mange,
how will any of us be free of rabbit?

Every hour I see them in the driveway,
under the porch, even eating the marigolds
meant to scare them off with poison.
When they used to hide at garden's edge,
now they are everywhere
as if to say with a joyful surge,
this time of scarcity was made for the twitching of a nose.

Neighbors on all sides of us now joke
about serving rabbit and I'm grateful for the memory,
coming up on foot to the Café Lapin near Lourmarin.
The only entrees:
Rabbit saddle with figs and spinach.
Boned rabbit stuffed with morels.
Rabbit marinated in cognac, thyme, shallots, truffles.
I had only enough for coffee and baguette.
The waiter brought a generous, steaming pot of rabbit stew.

From that time when I gobbled and stuffed
and sopped up a bowl
then backed away from a table with too few francs,
I want to commend the cloven rabbit
for entering the fire of nourishment.
You, of the shy flesh and blinding speed,
you, of the greatest numbers ever recorded,
thank you for your eating of the burnt summer grass,

thank you for listening in to our troubles,

thank you for your feeding of the smoldering world.

So Far As It Depends on You

It also depends on the dancer swiveling outside the pawn shop
of cheap guitars and semi-automatic weapons,
his thoracic cavity,
part cobra, part mongoose,
and given to the eternal stand-off at the end of the world.
It depends upon the blue-eyed enemy,
the kingfisher returning to the mouth of the river,
the bleached coral city and the lighthouse with a broken neck.
It depends upon the one lost paragraph
torn from the palace that reveals
who did the thing no one could imagine was possible.
It also depends on this journey
we never thought would be ours to take.
You and I, with no suitcase, no ticket, and no way back
will carry a shining leaf
to the center of the earth after the last tree is gone.

THE FUTURE

Since it's one of the few things left on earth we all share,
I'm thinking maybe
I should be kind and generous to whatever failings
it too will include.
What did the future mean to the ancients?
Plant something.
Pray for growth. Wait out disaster.
Become something new and ferocious.
This is what I set out to do every morning.
By evening, I feel defeated.
I look for bottles of wine, then remember I've thrown them out.
I remember Richard returning to Santorini
after thirty years of being away.
Many of his friends gathered at the same taverna
where he drank every night.
When they see him walk in with his daughter Rose,
they start singing and dancing.
With tears in his eyes,
he tells his companions God gave him 10,000 bottles of anything
and he happily drank them all,
and now he can drink no more,
but he wants them all to drink without him and live a long life,
much longer than any of them deserve.
He wants the future
to sprawl in beauty before them like the scarlet bougainvillea.
He wants them all to savor the three hearts
of the octopus they have ordered.
He wants the wine to soften any old hatreds and regrets.
He wants the future,
the one I can't imagine will be kind and generous to anyone,
to bring his friends only nouns and verbs
that will help them love and keep true to the fallen world.

THE OLD SEA TURTLE SAVES MY ASS
ON A SUMMER DAY IN MINNESOTA

Mid-August Minnesota sag. Every flower freighted
with more fade than it can hold.
                                Everything that's given
to the lag of heat will soon be gone: The hissing geese,
the tilting coneflower, the devoured milkweed.
                                All my life I have sought out turtles.
Walked them across sizzling highways or sat with them as they
buried themselves on the ocean floor. Why am I telling you this?

I laid down next to my flower bed to soak up the dying color
and remembered swimming off Maui, out to a curlicue of reef
where danger thrives. There,
                                I met a green turtle, old enough
to bear tumors around its eyes. We recognized one another,
both sick but still swimming. Our eyes held strong.
We sought out the salt distance of our lives come close.

I turned back and he headed out to sea or was it the other way
        around?

THE SECRET ROOM

For most, stealth is the last chance left.

Go into a secret room, shut the door.
That's what Matthew said of prayer.
No wonder I spend so much time alone,
looking for the orange slash of fox,
hoping to see her slip past the dogs.
She will fail before she succeeds
in bringing dinner home.
I will not be doing much today.
I will stay in the tub reading
the ancient Chinese poets,
grateful that war and famine
have never found me.
Like the days of lapis lazuli,
this is a dark time of imperial power.
It's hard to believe in anything but bandits.
If the fox comes your way,
please regard her as a figure of the present,
and not simply of the past
when everything we needed
was more fiercely praised before it was killed.

Free Diver at Makena Landing

What a gift to be on earth when all the failures
of the human family have arrived at once.
To swarms of locust, add freon.
To floating cities of plastic, add animal souvenirs.
To ancient streams diverted off the volcano, add tree thirst.
And let's not forget this addition...

Yesterday at Makena landing we met a free diver who told us
how he will deliver his proposal.
He will dive into the white tip shark cave, climb the ledge past
      them,
light a circle of candles,
then bring in his lovely and ask for her hand.
Danger. Purpose. Direction.
Once again, two people at the start of a world, making a plan
      in a cave.

In the Village of Swinging Lemons

I can't recall the name of the village of swinging lemons.
Can you? So richly juiced, the lemons became apples.

They grew everywhere on hillsides,
more than we could carry.

There wasn't much to do but read, walk, drink wine,
make love, pick figs, pears, gather quince off the ground.
The lemons?
                  We couldn't escape their pendulum.

Some were no bigger than an eyeglass. Others, softball size.
We found them all without hazard or hurry.

There were entire days when the sun rose
and set inside the rind of those found lemons.

We cared little for the politicians careening through streets
with bullhorns or for the knot of pilgrims streaming south.

We helped chase a girl's runaway pig, the color
of blue-black ink. We fell asleep in the shade of poplars,
dizzy with the scent of jasmine and wild celery.

I won't pretend we could ever find such a place again.

READING THE FAT LETTER

The lost thrill of the fat letter in the far sleeve of the mailbox.

Something unstoppable waiting there
like the sweep of the matador's cape
or the beam of a lighthouse besieged by combers,
the letter that knew how to track me
to the jag of a cornfield,
or behind the one pump gas station on Shields Avenue
to that town of five hellbent coal trains an hour
on a double crossover track headed for Toledo.

I want to call it the letter of unhoarded splendors,
unruly declarations, rusted gateways, a bite of sky,
lick of salt, the hint of an undressing,
the whisper conversation with everything unfinished
and there I am, greedy to unfold it,
pouring over the ink, what did I miss,
what did I find, how could so many deceits and subtractions,
so many delights and misdirections
be now available for the glow of a shiver examination,
lofting there in my hands, read it again, the letter
that belonged only to me like a broken bone that suddenly heals
after doctors said I would never walk again.

What of those letters you wrote late at night and never sent?

The letters you rushed to finish and never should have posted?

The letters you wrote, never sent and years later regretted not
        sending.

For now you believe their intended punishment or release
was essential to the story that hobbled the ones
who carried the alcoholic gene worming through a family?

If they live at all, as a knife and a wound that won't stop bleeding
or a kiss feathering between stations,
these letters must be yellowing in basement boxes,
or adrift in the garage in plastic tubs
and when you die, they too will all be set out at the curb,
those lowercase threads of longing and defeat, silence
          and clanging.

In the night's long middle skid,
I went looking for such a fat letter from my father,
the one he wrote when I was 16
where he rambled into a rare promise, to honor my convictions.
This while the news played on with body bags and taps
and he said I was right about one thing:
What war does best is keep making holes.

For a man who lived for the comics and gridirons,
this letter I couldn't find was a reach beyond
the buckeye trees and pink lemonade stands
to the hinges of one family's sorrow squeaking on an iron bed,
loud enough to drown out
the lips smacking over plates of buttered corn,
the slam of a porch door, someone running under a black hat
          of sky.

Like that Ukrainian folk tale where all the animals of the forest
are able to climb into one fallen mitten,
this letter made room for all the unresponsive scars,
Hagar the Horrible, the long-necked whiskey bottles
thrown overboard, as many raspberries as I could
shimmy off the fence and the bones, the many bones
          of my ancestors.

SEABOOTED

I looked at my father in his last bed and saw him there seabooted
in the cockpit, holding in his eyes how a hull slips under a wave
without losing its push into weather. He didn't hear my offerings
from a book he didn't believe in, so much as the flapping of cloth,
the leaning into it, the splash kick of wake boiling off the transom.
Like any ocean indifferent to suffering, he contained countless
      wrecks.
On many other nights, I had gone down into his waters to survey
the damage, salvage the proof, imagine some blood payment
I might add to the patina, but on that night, I put aside my
      vanishing
into the ink of some ancient faded ledger between us and stayed
at the low, wet rail and we made the turn through the eye
      of the wind
and together found the morning. One of us heard the ocean
      over the dune.

ELEGY FOR A BUCKEYE

I went all the way back to the beginning looking for a giant
on a quiet street in Ohio but it was gone and so were the spiny,
gold brown husks containing glossy nuts with circular eyes.

I always kept a buckeye in my pocket for any luck but bad,
and rubbed its smooth finish hoping it would shiver me through
my father's unhappiness with selling insurance for Metropolitan.

On the way home from school, I would listen to husks cracking,
the buckeyes falling for squirrels to lug off in their gaped mouths.
Food for winter? Isn't that our first and last theme? If I had one

right now, I could look into its varnished mahogany burl
and see my father thumbing a buckeye like a miniature football,
then launching it for a touchdown, my grandparents in Rye Beach

barefoot among the buckeyes to the beach for a last nude swim,
my Blue Angel cousin who crashed his jet must have held one
in his hands and used it, like me, to steer by when earthbound,

everyone in Ohio now distant from the trees they planted
to define them. Even the coalman conductor on a tight scream
clock who I waved to from my bike might have glimpsed

this beauty before he entered the steels mills in Chicago,
and thought for a moment he might lean against such a tree
and read a book. My memory of all this only as old as September

and young when compared to the Shawnee who named the tree
after its nut flicking a swale like a buck's eye. They are gone
along with the Delaware and Miami and every other tribe

that ever lived in Ohio where this tree once lived and laid out
a simple feast, or do I have it wrong and the eye of the tree
I climbed and loved still sees what is happening and holds on?

CITY IN THE TREES

It did not take that long to root this city beside the sea.
Not that long for it to leaf in.
No one now remembers when the sun
last scorched the back of their neck,
or when the tree shadows became the oldest of friends.
Can't find this city?
It could be just over there, as of yet unseen
from beneath the sea grape, banyan and Benjamin fig.
Did I mention the birds?
You can still hear the mynas and francolin
bringing their racket to the morning,
and the flycatchers and honeycreepers have now returned
from the steep valleys of the volcano,
and most everyone has given them favorite family names.

Why I've Gone Looking
for a Lime Green Tree Frog in Florida

When I think about what my brother came to.
A gash in his side that would never heal.

His own gizzard installed with a ventilation fan,
so he could stand the smell of his own flesh, rotting.

I can see him getting up from his bed to grill one more time.

I watch him through fogged AC glass,
standing in an apron,
holding a platter of meat.

The prehistoric June air swells around him.

He points upwards,
wavering with a fork, listing,
as if finally swooning from having been speared.

I rush outside to catch him,
but he's only looking at this lime green tree frog,
that lives in a cornice gap.

My brother says the frog has become a shipmate.

With sweat pouring off his head into his eyes,
he tells me neither of them is afraid to die.

Naked and poor in a body of smoke,
my brother makes me a last supper.

If the gate of heaven is open anywhere,
that lime green tree frog will know where to find it.

Who Can Know?

Who can know where the beginning and end change places,
when the hours themselves dissolve and gather again
in dreams, and you see in the shadows those you loved
so completely you couldn't imagine one day without them,
and yet they now exist somewhere without you—or
did they ever leave the fierce pull of your arms?

Who can turn away from those few lingering nights,
now gone, when you discovered the rare sweetness
of her skin, how it seemed with each lick to guide you
farther into that stand of peaches overlooking a harbor
where a sunken tender was slowly being raised
from the tangled mud of a storm from the distant north?

Who can deny there's something about us, vanishing,
that travels beyond this place — our blood and bones
mostly water, all of it seeking greater depth, the end of us
starting again somewhere unseen to pull back and rise
into the next breaking wave, where you and I read
our books on a beach while a ship scores the horizon.

COMPASS ROSE

After you wet a finger and hold in your mouth
the shards of bone found in your mother's ash,
then set that gray out upon the tide,
you can't go home and shut the door
and pretend you are separate
from the thread connecting every tide to every moon.
You can't pretend your rent or your grocery bill
is your demon or the lock on your door will protect you.
You can't pretend your pillow is your best friend
and by morning everything will be better.
After such a taste on your tongue,
no house can hold you
and only the sea will provide,
after such ash and bone in your mouth.

HIGH RIDGE ON THE NORTH SHORE

How can we not walk out on a high ridge ending at a sea cliff
and there find a trail tucked under strangler figs,
the trail hugging a stream bed
leading down to a bay of blown white rollers
where it can't be safe to swim unless you are a turtle or tiger shark,

and yet to walk beside this salt clamor
is to be in a world
where the belief in the wearing down and the seeding again
somewhere else is not hard to acquire.

I'm sure winter will find us again
with its repertoire of withering conclusions,
but today, right now,
with the snap of the afternoon Trades in our pace,
there are no doors and windows set to rattle,
no need for the shivering of bones and a psalm to swear by.

You might even say
we could be these monster swells from Alaska,
the hope of something reaching another island and then another.

THE FIG TREE IN LOURMARIN

Out for one of my walks before the heat returned,
I remember meeting this fig tree.
What I can't remember now is whether this meeting occurred
before or after I found Camus's grave:
That small, simple stone affair overgrown with grass.
I do recall standing outside the pink door
of the silk worm loft where he lived and smiling
at how he could almost reach across his street and touch a church.
What else?
My brother sent out his nightly
notes from Chemo Brain and I walked with such guilt
even though he begged me to go to fucking France.
And my marriage?
I couldn't find its fig tree, its pink door,
its church, only its stone gate shadowed by tall grass.
I know I was crying in the fire of August
and looking for a fig tree the grave keeper told me
was so abundant it could chutney an army,
and I did find it beyond the cemetery,
this lone tree
with limbs spreading wide and low,
dressed in the ruin of summer,
the ground of its standing littered with rotting husks.
I pulled apart the branches, ducked inside a sticky cavity,
and picked a purple fig.
Not one wrapped in ham, chèvre and dipped in honey.
Not one sautéed in butter and spread on bruschetta
and dribbled with balsamic,
sold on the corner where the Algerian lived,
but a naked one
with its head in the sun and its feet in water,
and I held the flesh of its long unstoppable life in my mouth
and rolled its crunchy seeds on my tongue.
In the beginning was the word,
the moist, luscious, solitary word, and the word was fig.

Dream of the State with the Prettiest Name

I'm in the brackish, burning kudzu middle of Florida.
A vulture feasting in the road is late to rise
and smacks my windshield but does not die.
Its severed eyes stare into my eyes
and I have to pull over because of the blood and feathers.
This is fifty years ago,
America at war, someone I knew already dead.
I open the car door to the fierce obbligato of swamp hum
to clean the windshield.
I'm engulfed by smoke.
I don't clean anything.
I get back in. Sit there waiting.
When the smoke starts to tear away in wisps,
I see black men by the road chained at the ankle,
working a ditch line,
nothing in their eyes.
A white man with a pump shotgun leans into my window,
This is no place to stop, son.
I say something about the smoke.
Move along now. You might just make it.
I start my car, pull away slowly, glancing over my shoulder
at the black men who never look up.
And the bright orange, heart-shaped cockle shell is still there
        in Florida.

Something Magnificent

After picking up milk and eggs, then walking through a parking lot,
we can forget that something magnificent and invisible
is always with us,
the way the unseen mother humpback
is always somewhere beneath a swell teaching her calf
how to hold its air longer with each dive.

For the last month of her life,
I slept in the room next to hers,
but on her last night, I slept on the floor beside her bed,
listened to her foamed, mucous expulsions.
This was the first and only time I stayed alone with my mother.
I was afraid of her rasp and drag.
How everything strangled in her was also in me.
Difficulty, death, everything.
I lay there remembering how nothing is what it seems.
Her small last room was really an ocean.
Every time I put my head under water, I heard the giants
        and their young.

FOR THE HOUSE WREN
WHO LIVES IN MY FATHER'S SAILING BOOT

How many times have I started a new day sitting in old darkness
waiting for light to inch back along the leggy, twisted lilacs,
eager for the house wren, nesting in my dead father's black rubber
sailing boot, to zip line the mulberry with its tangled song?

Not many of us will figure out how to save our miserable lives
at the last possible turn and work that rescue into a repertoire.
Most will stagger forward with our precious wounds
and make them worse. You know this is how the story goes,
so does the wren.
                    The song the wren releases from her small,
plain, brown body, how best to describe all that it can hold?

THE FOX HAS RISEN FROM HER WINTER HOLLOW

The old reprobate in me hates to give up this much ground to gospel,
but everything I said was my sworn enemy
has turned out to be my friend.
                                        Take time, for example.
How often have I claimed time cared nothing for my story,
my beautiful plans, and so I've wasted a thousand nights
threading the darkness with my knotted string
of baleful disappointments.
                                Let's say this another way:
The fox has risen out of her winter hollow like Lazarus of Bethany,
her coat a sickly splotch of gray and orange,
the way you imagine a man four days dead might look.
What did Jesus say to sisters, Mary and Martha?
Unbind him.
                        Sometimes we become hidden in our grave clothes
long before we are dead and we wish someone would plead
with us to come out into the greater life. *Unbind me*
from this clock, this calendar, the little arc of my life.

Once you clang your spoon against the bars of your cell,
and make the best music you can,
then you're ready to hear something even more insistent:

                        Your own voice says, I am unclothed,
undecayed, untethered. Where can I go? *Anywhere the fox goes.*
Anywhere Lazarus goes. You are no longer a man dressed for sorrow.

TRILL

Up in a cloud valley, in a parking lot, in my bed,
I hear the trill of the zebra dove.
There is not much left we haven't cut down, hauled off.
Not much we haven't fished out and muddied,
and still the tremolo holds from somewhere I can't see,
the dove in the marrow of first light,
taking nothing for her journey, wearing no shoes, looking for seeds.

SAINT FRANCIS, SHE SAID

She said death would alter her view of the olive trees,
and the relationship would not end.
Love means your flesh will be torn off
yet you will not die.
She made it sound romantic.
Just another spill of language that nicks you at a precipice.
I knew better.
The surge of emptiness like a knife at the throat.
The kicking of the ankle bones.
All of it waiting you out.
She said she had struck a truce with pain and beauty,
The two faces of God.
I had a need to know this agreement.
Saint Francis, she said, would sometimes weep for days,
even after the Sultan of the Fifth Crusade
let him return to Italy and Francis cut a deal with his wolf.
Weeping all the time
with the ferocious and the small,
never turning away from the boundaries that dissolve us.
Talking like that about a saint,
she could have been one of her olive trees
set back on a turn of collapsed coast where the sea never sleeps.

Stay With Me, Here in the Garden

I rescued a snake from a flattening in the road.
Already nicked by a tire,
it squirmed and spun and could not reach the grass,
the motor of its serpentine coils all but spent.
In the speed and drift of July,
blood wept out of its skin.
This jade green beauty with a yellow stripe
would not live much longer.
I am no great friend to all that crawls
with dust on its belly
but I looked into its blue eyes
knowing I had to ask this snake a question about the garden.
Whether it was worth dying for.
We could have been two meteors meeting for the first time.

BLACK DOG UNDER THE PERSIMMON

The ladder resting against the trunk has always
been ready to hoist someone to fetch fruit
from the tangled upper limbs. You might say
the persimmon will live as long as the picker,
then it, too, must fall or rot from within after carrying
so much autumn. The black dog, however,
will always be here sleeping in the sun, the dog
that everyone has seen and no one can say
where it came from, that dog with no name.
Black dog, orange globe, ladder in the cloud.

THE SPIRIT PENS A WINTER LETTER TO THE ENEMY

The wise ones say just consent to everything that comes
your way no matter what it is, and presto,
the cane toad in you,
the one with venom blooming
in your shoulder blades
can now gather as a finch on a raspberry stalk.

With apologies to wisdom,
I can't accept the tooth and claw of so many things.
This morning it's the beaver
who cuts down another tree in the night.

Cottonwood, peachleaf willow, dogwood,
all my friends now dead
and lying face down in the river.

How can I not go to war one more time?

DREAM OF LOVERS ON THE STONE ARCH BRIDGE DURING PANDEMIC

Most everyone on the bridge tonight is moving slowly
like a reptile in cobwebs.

Everyone of a certain age
given over to some ancient consideration
wondering if they should be here
without a dagger or crossbow.

Here so far above the water
in a cemetery of hidden glances and fatal viscosities.

Everyone notched in shadow
like they have just read a trunk of crumpled letters
and tossed them into the Mississippi boil.

Everyone playing solitaire by the spill of an oil lamp.
Everyone climbing worn steps.

Everyone but the lovers who have brought
their teasing, their jewels, their tattoos, their bedrooms.

See the door of that blouse swing open.
See that fling of a wet kiss.

See the nausea and the vertigo in the elders and that other thing
lifted in the arms,
the gold nail of lightning in a spill of long, black hair.

Port Aransas

It is said of Christ he never laughed.

That he saw how the wheel
caught the sparrow and the dove
and he found nothing funny about what had to happen next.

Here on this rawhide beach in the south horn of Texas
with whitecap horses on parade,
the world has already ended gleefully
in a gridlock of aftermarket, off-road, jacked up monsters
rafted up and sporting
Skull & Cross Bone pirate flags:
Go topless. Go guns. Go America. Come & Take It.

A pregnant woman knee deep in rollers,
turns sideways to shelter her womb.
The waves ride over belly, wetting her face.
Her husband wades out to her with another child in his arms.

The new young family in the old rough land splashing it up.

How have we come this far? How will we go on from here?

The donkey ride into town must have brought out a smile.

A Tree Becomes a Room

Thick of girth with flaking scales,
the gingko had seen emperors come and go
through wars, flood, famine.

It had lost its yellow leaves
and replaced them with green again.

Yuan Mei decided to shelter its trunk
by spending more time
watching over it.
He called this place,
A Tree Becomes a Room.

The Taoist poets might welcome this time behind closed doors
to visit again forgotten poems,
unfinished garden plans.
Wherever they are,
they are always climbing,
sweeping a mountain path with their footsteps.

No, that's a lie. That's too pretty.
On many days, they can't write.
They can't speak.
They can't put on their shoes.
They can do nothing more than sit for a time in the gingko room.

Dream of a Cottonwood

It's a soft wood with a hard eye.
It's a darkness fueled by the blood of crows and owls.
It's the smell of Dakota wind spit over shale, gully, rolling grass.

Its roots reach down below the shovels of dead Scottish settlers,
past the gopher and chipmunk tunnels and the crisscross
      of conduit and sewer.
It holds one entire street in its muscled torque.

It's hard not to feel strongly about this tree,
the way you do about a sheriff left alone with scripture.
In May, its sap pellets eat car paint. June brings trampled tufts
      of snow.

Giant spears snap from its crown in July thunder.
In September, it showers tons of silver dollar leaves
into gutters and drainpipes. In January, it throws shadow bones
      on snow,

and lives as a thing aggrieved by the tongue of winter.
It is our Mount Vesuvius. One day it will crush homes in a tremor
      of joy.
Just the other night, I got a peek at heaven stalking this cloud-tree

with rain-claws shining. A straight-line wind peeled off ribs
of inner sheathing yet when I looked up,
the tree buffed stronger from the storm.

Two men squared off in the street to fight about the limb
      wreckage.
Why hasn't it been cut down, one man demanded.
The other defended the cottonwood's claim to the neighborhood.

The police came. Nothing happened that would be written
      on the furl of its bark.
It was here before the men were born.
It will remain a century after they are dead.

It doesn't care who loves or hates it.
It is cut. It grows taller. It dies. It lives on.
It stands up inside the fence of lightning to grab the voltage
      with its fingers.

IN THE AFTERLIFE OF THE GARDEN
OF ACCOMMODATION, A MEMORY HOLDS FORTH

Consider the brightness of my offering: sandalwood, pear, catalpa.

When the planting of apricot and pecan was akin to caring for elders.

When the placement of stones sprang from listening to the rain.

When the pulling of a weed released the long-awaited, *Yes, Yes.*

When walking in silence was the only way to oil the far gate.

I remember this much: The life of a garden is one of continual
    assault.

Glamour and plunder and the long reach of the November wind.

Like others before me, I took root at the tail end of a declining age.

FIRE

Then you said, what things don't catch fire?

The ocean ignites. Mountains in snow smolder on.

We flicker here before we enter the smudge of ash.

Am I remembering any of this the way you meant it?

Right here, your face in my hands, and your mouth

seeking mine, you tell me, it's never too late

for the cow bell to call, never too late to walk

the high goat trail into town. Unmistakable pleasures.

Impossible clarity. The gravel throat of the river.

The hot, thin trail of planets, unexplained fevers.

Jailors, presidents, the fiery worm of our numbered days.

Days of Joy

On a hilltop lit with angelica, yarrow and ironweed,
I saw merrily and not so merrily the wine bottles,
shoes, gloves, jackets, underwear ripped away.
I saw the lost brother. The unreachable neighbor.
The unfinished child war at the forever border.
How quickly everything I care for will be forgotten
after my stake in the ground will be torn loose.

I could tell you I set my mind on the things above
and the things of the earth found me wanting.
I could tell you I saw the flowering and I failed
to break open the buried seed or I could tell you
I kept the unlikely peace as long as I could, then
I moved on just as perplexed as when I arrived,
but for the hour we met and the days of joy that followed.

Here at hand. Within reach. Available for work. Now.
Light of the milk slapping the bucket from the cow I just met
at five in the morning in the far reach of the northeast kingdom.
Light of the apple tree pruned just enough in late winter
to throw a cat through while your hands and feet make numb.
Light of the duck pond across the street from 38th and Chicago
where the neck bones of a man are pinned to the pavement.
Light of the ocean with the heads torn off of the outer waves
so the spume can send an unwanted kiss to the shipwrecked.
Light of the moment just before the final unveiling comes
and the face of the vanishing one gathers the look of a pearl.
Light of the hook jigging bottom in search of the mouth
of a fish fat enough to feed an entire family for a week.
Light of the 139th Psalm braided with darkness with no telling
where shade enters and the other climbs the morning wing.
Light of the smoke that lingers in the reek of a slaughterhouse
and makes you look again into the fires of your own choosing.
Light of the boarded window that reminds you that the lamp
has not yet come to every street in the city set up on the hill.
Light of the salt that tightens the strands of flour so the bread
can stand up in the morning to greet the earthen brown and gold.
Light of four-twelve in the morning when the thrush and the dove
decide again that any stray, pot-bellied song is better than none.

HERE FOR NOW

There is no explaining Miami.

The double-wide Cuban cigar cases in the gelato store.
The nippled bikini mannikins.
The ghost tankers hanging offshore like barracudas
in a mist of hallucination.

Much has been written about the old time movie stars
who camped out here in the Art Deco hotels
in between the flash powder of wedding photos.
Rita, Marlene, Marilyn, Joan, Clark.
You know you still miss them.
Less has been noted
about the hidden colonnade of tamanu trees.
The bark like the scales of a dragon.
The leaves offering a cloaked entrance to another world.
The nuts containing a green oil said to heal any wound.

Only here on this glam watermark, that one day will be a reef,
can you find more tamanu nuts
than you could ever carry.

When I picked one up, I heard the faint rattle
of the nut over the salsa in the street
and I thought I could go on into whatever was coming next.

In Praise of Failure in My Seventh Decade

Today I went looking for a word
but it did not come looking for me
so we remained lost to one another.
I've not given up on what it might offer,
the same way I won't give up on a tattoo
repeating its message from beneath a sleeve
that balloons next to me at the café.
Look, I lived long enough to know
when you seek something out, mostly
you only find the restless ghost of it
and not the thing it once was,
but someone has to keep failing
to catch it with a pen or sword,
failing to hear the meadow and sky
of its earlier travels, failing the splendor,
the ragged scar, someone has to hold
the loose page and wait out the night
and the next day, hoping this one word
will open the door and step through.

YOU THERE IN BED, STILL SLEEPING

Any minute now, I am going to fall more and more in love
with every nail in the board. The stinkbug on the ceiling.
The mouse in the ceiling joist. The linden that died over winter.
Any minute now, the spring, that will never arrive, will be my
      friend
and I will welcome the angel of the flaming sword who keeps
me from returning home. Any minute now, I will stop writing
letters to the governor and telling him where he has failed
to meet his obligations and I will gladly sit under the rain fly
of everything I don't understand. Any minute now I assure you
everything in my world, and yours, will be regarded as sacrament.
The locked door, the open window, you there in bed, still sleeping.

BREAKFAST IN BED

What is our business here on this sullied plain,
where the oldest roads
were once called rivers
and no one traveled anywhere without asking them first?
Maybe it's just tears.
That's what we must be here for.
Tears at the beginning.
Tears at the end.
Everything now begins with the end of something.
That's not the whole story, right?
There was laughter too in the morning.
That time, for example, when young Cory
sent a stream of pee off the balcony
and we heard sizzling on the iron stove below
and thought ling cod chipatis were on their way to us in bed.

THE ARMADA

I'm on good terms with the morning and the evening.
Less so with the long afternoon
when everything stalls in the court of the sun,
and I have a testy, sometimes
combative relationship with the soft, unbounded night.
This is disturbing because as a boy
I took pride in being able to sleep
on a boat, park bench, bus stop, anywhere.
I knew then what I can't seem to know now.
That we are continuous between waking and sleeping
like a breeze at the curtain,
or a goat on a mountain trail over the ocean
and not for a moment confined by the day or the night.
How can I even offer this reflection
given what I dredge up before dawn?
From my pillow, a visitation from a dead friend.
I saw him again hectoring on
about the sorry world that refuses to grow up.
I wasn't fooled by this stage act.
I knew he was talking about me.
How even now, when it's fair to say I am old,
I want more of the day, less of the night.
I want the morning to show me to the door.
To watch the geese sailing across the harbor
in that single file armada they do.
Maybe you too have seen it?
How quietly it steers into any long-threatening blast of wind.

WHAT IF

Given our small pocket of days to fill, what if we went up into
        that valley
and over that mountain, what if we only told fables about animals,
legends about flowers, what if we joined the wind that defeated
        an army,
what if our most trusted confidantes were trees and stones
        and ferns
and we were surrounded on all sides by almost nothing that had
        a name,
would this be a death by solitude and inconvenience or something
        else?
I know how to weep for my loved ones and they know how
        to weep for me,
but who wakes up every day weeping for those places that have not
        yet been
platted and deeded by survey? Who still says, a thousand years ago,
one morning, I heard this bird, then I followed it and then I
        disappeared?

Regarding that Lily
Found Nowhere Else on Earth

I almost forgot to mention, the grasshoppers, the ones with
    a vertical face,
and a swollen thorax that always give you a start, have become
more bold with the uptick in flame. The other day at Kowalski's
    Market,
between the watermelons and raspberries, I saw one hopping about
as if to say with those little dancing shoes, *all this too will soon be mine.*

I could be wrong about them as I am about so many things, but now
I see there everywhere nibbling down the leaf end of things.
I would like to say, like Rumi, you are welcome here, all of you, in a
    swarm of leaping,
but they remind me so much of my own devouring. How I want
    and want
just a little more of this life. Eating until I can eat no more, then
    moving on
for a glimpse of the dwarf trout lily that grows here and nowhere
    else on earth.

Dirt & Water

What did I do here?

I went out into big water when no one else would go.

I let the wind soften my grimace.

I was always in school but I never once met the teacher.

I sought love, recognition, intoxication.
Equilibrium was beyond my reach.

I was surprised by many things.
That love can pillage and soothe in the same breath.
That fear always brings its own fever.

That dirt and water are the only friends who never disappoint.

Fooling around with flowers, boats and trees.
Mining the darkness under the finger nails.
Not much of a contribution.

Still, I saw this miracle at dawn:

What stands in the dirt and what flows to the sea
are married under the sun
and always waiting for the next apprenticeship.

What the Spirit Knows, the Body Remembers
At the Foot of a Bed

The wind has brought a flame from the south.
That's about all I know
and death is not about failure.
There was a time when I thought otherwise.
Even watching salmon stuck at a waterfall,
or a bear sprawled in an apple tree,
I thought this was a failure.
To climb into the tang of an old hunger
and never touch the sky.
There was a time when I would say
If I have a problem, the problem must be you.
There was another time
when I was convinced the body
and spirit live on opposite sides of the room
and only at death do they lay together.
Watching my mother inch around
the foot of her bed, everything changed.
I had never seen such mingling,
the breath of her, the smoke of her,
seeking the bathroom,
this long voyage to the toilet,
a study in slowness, climbing, falling,
a world away from safety,
then the pinched-eye trudge back to bed.
She could have been a returning salmon
or a late October bear with a wild flame
pouring out of her thick coat.
There was never another time like this.

LETTER TO WANG WEI

The number of gasbags and bullies has not diminished
since I last wrote to you.
They are now talking even faster
and everywhere I walk I have to cross the border of their spit.
I'm afraid I will never live to see the empire return
to peace so I wanted to ask you
how you managed to keep company with the clouds and dogwood
without disappointment
turning your last years into a busy rebellion.

I struggle every day to make sense
of the leeches of addition and subtraction.
All those tickets sold by the orchestras of deceit.
Everything that's clutched by the left or right hand.

I wanted to tell you that the night gibbons
you spoke of at Mount Hua have almost no future now
but the orioles in Minnesota are still
hanging their ornament nests in the sugar maples.

As you suggested, most mornings I am up long before dawn.
The house is quiet although I can hear the cars
already swarming into the city,
the heartbeat of their wheels the most prevalent sound,
so loud now I often don't hear the rain or the wind
          or the distant church bells.

WING WALKING

Staying power. The ant and the bee, they have it.
The wind and the rain do not require more confidence.
Mary standing with Christ at the cross.
She is not going anywhere until the blood stops running.
What's the lesson here? Stay right where you are?
Almost everything now is sooner than later.
It takes so much just to be here watching our unwinding.
Today, it's a friend given two more months to live.
I told him I'm not going anywhere, but it's not true.
I have a trip planned to an island to see my sister
who is also old and who challenged me on my 70th,
to go wing walking into the spin of the sky, to stay
there inside the loops and climbs, feel again
the weightlessness, the heaviness, the scream of it all.

LITTLE WINDOW

I was rich last night sleeping next to you
and bought this home in a banana gulch
between Makawao and Haiku.
The stars were so close I pulled one down
and used it to better see this home
with no front door and only one little window.
I wiped off the smudge of glass
with my shirt and looked inside
where we would be living from now on.
Small as it was
and hidden beneath the fronds,
this place would hold us under the darkest of skies.
We would be happy there, you said,
with that one window and the stars looking in.

Afternoon at the Mouth of the Elwha River Released from Its Dam

Let's go to the end of the road on the wrong side of the river.
Let's sit at the mouth and watch the dog shine face of harbor seals
and the knife of the orcas feared by almost everything born in salt.
Let's not spend another minute inside the marrow of our tragedies.
You know the list: a fortune lost, a bad leg, brothers in a feud,
a father who drank whiskey at dawn, a mother with a ragged tongue,
a world at war with trees and fish and bears seeking the ripe apple.
Let's just admit we walked into long shadow when we owned the sun.
Let's sleep for an hour in the midst of the driftwood and salmon
      bones.
Let's wake to this unburdening, our turn at the surge of an empty cup.
Let's just do it all now while we are gathered here at the end of the
      road
with a river released from its concrete fortress no one believed
      could ever fall.

BESIDES THIS, YOU KNOW WHAT TIME IT IS

Romans

Besides this, it's the time when I worry
the most prized corner of my monologue will never calve
and drop into a colossal sea of unknowing,
so I can begin again the impossible dialogue with the world.
It must be the time when someone I love
is about to arrive while someone else is ready to leave.
David, for example, my dear brother,
inside his unmoored chemo brain,
when Lynda told him he was dying, said,
Fuck. Really? So soon?
How else can I say this?
It's the time when the moon is a tin cup in a whiskey lip
and some ruminant blend of delight and dread
sits with me in my 3 a.m. kitchen.
And now since the thought of food has entered this poem,
the reluctant Yes I live for
has yet to break bread with the insistent No.
I swear this is when all the unrecorded orchestras
are lit in the devoted cordgrass,
the foghorn has set down the length of its tether,
and the time has come to listen in,
or the time has already come and gone. You decide?

On the Other Side of Elegy

Maybe it's not too late for the flamingo.
Not too late for the rhino and snow leopard.
Misfortune here. Misfortune there.
Not everyone meets the lord in a lightning bolt.
I will never give up on slowness.
The squeaking of our flesh under apple blossoms.
Big fish gliding under lily pads.
Think of the farthest of the far islands,
the plovers who sail there,
their backs flecked with gold,
how long it takes to trace
the shadow wing of an entire ocean.
Though I may lose the blade of my pretty teeth,
watch the rain disappear from summer,
I won't surrender a single corner
of our dust and your salt on my tongue,
and that dog named Charlie
who must believe paradise is already here,
on the other side of elegy.

Narrow, Dead-End Road

There is a world on a narrow, dead-end road above the sea
where you think you can always start over
no matter how old you've become,
a world forgotten and always known,
just there, forever out of reach.
This is where you imagine you would like to spend
the number of days you have left
inside a pocket of green looking out at a sliver of blue.

SEED IN A JAR

You will die before finishing your bridge to the moon.
Until then, how far can you tumble toward a small,
bright introduction? Always good to spend time
with rivers and mountains and the downpour of stars.
Still, more negotiation to be done with the thieves
who come early, stay late. You know their names.
I hope just carrying a seed in a jar is enough.

About That Love Letter to the Earth

Every morning I rise in the dark to write another love letter.
I write of the sprawling Russian sage
at the end of my driveway, how the bumblebees
stay with it until the pollen blows out in September.
I write about sailboats that never leave their moorings.
About brother/sister dogs from the pound,
about kites, stone arch bridges,
plumeria, fat, uneaten eggplant,
the goldfinch I once met looking for an island,
and Amy who wanders our road
looking for her room at the Starfish apartments.
I tell myself from the edge of my chair,
the future of the human race is not set in the stone
of our nasty and brutish ways. No matter
the million dead ends we have laid down,
no matter the fires and the fools
who would take all the wreckage for themselves,
I tell myself the universe is still looking out
for this blue thread woven into a vast tunnel of stars.
I know it seems silly to be writing such a letter in the dark,
a letter few people will ever read
but it's all I know to do.
Tell the earth, as long as I am able,
I will keep coming back to my chair in the dark.
To hunt, to wrestle, to pray. To open my eyes after sleep
    and have a look around.

J.P. White has published essays, articles, fiction, reviews, interviews and poetry in many places including *The Nation, The New Republic, The Gettysburg Review, Agni Review, Catamaran, APR, Salamander, Catamaran, North American Review, Shenandoah, The Georgia Review, Southern Review, The Massachusetts Review, Water-Stone, The New York Times, Willow Springs, Crazyhorse, Peripheries*, and *Poetry* (Chicago). White is the author of five previous books of poems, and a novel, *Every Boat Turns South. Norah Bow*, a novel, is forthcoming in 2024 from Regal House Publishing.

THE WHITE PINE PRESS POETRY PRIZE

Vol. 28: *The Tree Becomes a Room* by J. P. White.
Selected by Danusha Laméris.

Vol. 27: *Blue If Only I Could Tell You* by Richard Tillinghast.
Selected by Joe Wilkins.

Vol. 26: *The Book of Mirrors* by Yun Wang.
Selected by Jennifer Kwon Dobbs.

Vol. 25: *Aflame* by Gary McDowell.
Selected by Sean Thomas Dougherty.

Vol. 24: *Our Age of Anxiety* by Henry Israeli.
Selected by Kathleen McGookey.

Vol. 23: *Secure Your Own Mask* by Shaindel Beers.
Selected by Alan Michael Parker.

Vol. 22: *Bread From a Stranger's Oven* by Janlori Goldman.
Selected by Laure-Anne Bosselaar.

Vol. 21: *The Brighter House* by Kim Garcia.
Selected by Jericho Brown.

Vol. 20: *Some Girls* by Janet McNally.
Selected by Ellen Bass.

Vol. 19: *Risk* by Tim Skeen.
Selected by Gary Young.

Vol. 18: *What Euclid's Third Axiom Neglects to Mention About Circles*
by Carolyn Moore.
Selected by Patricia Spears Jones.